The Wilder
Collaboration
Factors Inventory

Assessing Your Collaboration's Strengths and Weaknesses

Paul W. Mattessich, Ph.D.
Marta Murray-Close, B.A.
Barbara R. Monsey, M.P.H.
Wilder Research Center

Fieldstone Alliance is committed to strengthening the perfor-
mance of the nonprofit sector. Through the synergy of its consult-
ing, training, publishing, and research and demonstration projects,
Fieldstone Alliance provides solutions to issues facing the nonprofit sector. Fieldstone Alliance was formerly a department of
the Amherst H. Wilder Foundation. If you would like more information about Fieldstone Alliance and our services, please contact
Fieldstone Alliance, 60 Plato Boulevard East, Suite 150, Saint
Paul, MN 55107, 651-556-4500

We hope you find this book useful! For information about other
Fieldstone Alliance publications, please contact:

Fieldstone Alliance Publishing Center
60 Plato Boulevard East
Suite 150
Saint Paul, MN 55107
800-274-6024
www.FieldstoneAlliance.org

Edited by Vincent Hyman
Designed by Rebecca Andrews

Manufactured in the United States of America
Second printing, July 2005

ISBN 978-0-94006-934-3

*Funding for the research that underpins this inventory
was provided (at various times) by The David and Lu-
cile Packard Foundation, the Amherst H. Wilder Foundation, The Saint Paul Foundation, the United Ways of
both Saint Paul and Minneapolis, and the Minneapolis
Foundation.*

THE WILDER COLLABORATION FACTORS INVENTORY is based on research conducted by Wilder Research Center to determine what ingredients make for a successful collaboration. The researchers identified twenty factors that influence the success of a collaboration. These factors have been reviewed by other researchers and employed by numerous practitioners of collaboration. For full details on the factors and the research, see our related publication, *Collaboration: What Makes It Work, Second Edition,* available from Fieldstone Alliance, 1-800-274-6024, or visit www.FieldstoneAlliance.org.

How to Use This Inventory

Use the inventory when planning a collaborative initiative as well as after a collaboration has started. The inventory can be taken by a small group of leaders, or it can be given to many people representing all collaborating organizations. However you administer it, you can use the inventory to:

- **Assess the likelihood of success *before* beginning collaborative work.**

  For this use, the group's planning committee should take The Wilder Collaboration Factors Inventory before or at the very beginning of a collaborative. This helps the committee know where their strengths lie and what areas they need to improve before startup.

- **Analyze the strengths and weaknesses of your collaborative venture.**

  The Wilder Collaboration Factors Inventory can prompt discussion, planning, and improved management of a collaborative group at any point during the initiative. Take time during a large group meeting for members to rate the collaboration. Use the results to spur discussion of the collaboration.

Administering the Inventory

We have had success administering the inventory at a full meeting of the collaborative, or via mail. Both methods have advantages and drawbacks.

Distribute and administer the inventory at a collaborative meeting. Have meeting attendees complete the inventory individually. Then calculate the scores for each partner organization and for the group as a whole during the meeting. The scores direct attention to the collaboration's strengths and weaknesses, and to differences in the ways individual organizations rate the collaboration.

This approach is excellent for spurring discussion, but it can be difficult to administer the instrument and tally scores in a reasonable amount of time, and the collaborative group misses input from absent members.

Mail the inventory to members and discuss the results at your next meeting. Mailing is a good way to solicit input from large numbers of people at any point during the initiative. A mailing can include all relevant people, is not as dependent on schedules as are meetings, and allows people to complete the inventory independently, at their convenience. Scores can then be calculated prior to the meeting at which they are discussed. Mailing has some drawbacks, though. Mailed inventories may result in poor response rates, especially among busy people, and mailings do not lead to the immediate interaction and feedback that occurs at meetings.

The Wilder Collaboration Factors Inventory

This questionnaire can help your group inventory its strengths on the factors that research has shown are important for the success of collaborative projects. The questionnaire is designed for use by people who are planning or participating in collaborative projects.

There are no right or wrong answers. Your opinion is important, even if it is very different from the opinions of others. When your group sees the results, you all will learn how people feel—whether they all feel the same or different about the questions.

Unless your group has decided to put names on the questionnaires, your answers will not be associated with your name and will be grouped with the answers of others.

Instructions

Please follow the instructions *exactly*. They are very simple:

1. Read each item.

2. Circle the number that indicates how much you agree or disagree with each item.

3. Do not skip any items.

4. Return your form as instructed by your group leader or facilitator.

You might want to do something a bit differently, but we have learned from experience that your group will get the most benefit if you fill out the questionnaire as the instructions describe. Some special situations:

"Don't know"

If you feel you don't know how to answer an item, or that you don't have an opinion, circle the "neutral" response, the number 3.

Opinion falls "in between two numbers"

If you feel that your opinion lies in between two numbers, pick the lower of the two. Do not put a mark in between the two numbers; and do not circle both of them. For example, if you feel your opinion lies between 1 and 2, circle the 1.

The Wilder Collaboration Factors Inventory

_____   _____
Name of Collaboration Project   _Date_

If you have been asked to provide your name or the name of your organization, please do so below.

_____   _____
Respondent Name   _Organization_

Include your name or the name of your organization on the line above only if instructed to do so.

Statements about Your Collaborative Group

Factor	Statement	Strongly Disagree	Disagree	Neutral, No Opinion	Agree	Strongly Agree
History of collaboration or cooperation in the community	1. Agencies in our community have a history of working together.	1	2	3	4	5
	2. Trying to solve problems through collaboration has been common in this community. It's been done a lot before.	1	2	3	4	5
Collaborative group seen as a legitimate leader in the community	3. Leaders in this community who are not part of our collaborative group seem hopeful about what we can accomplish.	1	2	3	4	5
	4. Others (in this community) who are not part of this collaboration would generally agree that the organizations involved in this collaborative project are the "right" organizations to make this work.	1	2	3	4	5
Favorable political and social climate	5. The political and social climate seems to be "right" for starting a collaborative project like this one.	1	2	3	4	5
	6. The time is right for this collaborative project.	1	2	3	4	5
Mutual respect, understanding, and trus	7. People involved in our collaboration always trust one another.	1	2	3	4	5
	8. I have a lot of respect for the other people involved in this collaboration.	1	2	3	4	5
Appropriate cross section of members	9. The people involved in our collaboration represent a cross section of those who have a stake in what we are trying to accomplish.	1	2	3	4	5
	10. All the organizations that we need to be members of this collaborative group have become members of the group.	1	2	3	4	5
Members see collaboration as in their self-interest	11. My organization will benefit from being involved in this collaboration.	1	2	3	4	5

Factor	Statement	Strongly Disagree	Disagree	Neutral, No Opinion	Agree	Strongly Agree
Ability to compromise	12. People involved in our collaboration are willing to compromise on important aspects of our project.	1	2	3	4	5
Members share a stake in both process and outcome	13. The organizations that belong to our collaborative group invest the right amount of time in our collaborative efforts.	1	2	3	4	5
	14. Everyone who is a member of our collaborative group wants this project to succeed.	1	2	3	4	5
	15. The level of commitment among the collaboration participants is high.	1	2	3	4	5
Multiple layers of participation	16. When the collaborative group makes major decisions, there is always enough time for members to take information back to their organizations to confer with colleagues about what the decision should be.	1	2	3	4	5
	17. Each of the people who participate in decisions in this collaborative group can speak for the entire organization they represent, not just a part.	1	2	3	4	5
Flexibility	18. There is a lot of flexibility when decisions are made; people are open to discussing different options.	1	2	3	4	5
	19. People in this collaborative group are open to different approaches to how we can do our work. They are willing to consider different ways of working.	1	2	3	4	5
Development of clear roles and policy guidelines	20. People in this collaborative group have a clear sense of their roles and responsibilities.	1	2	3	4	5
	21. There is a clear process for making decisions among the partners in this collaboration.	1	2	3	4	5
Adaptability	22. This collaboration is able to adapt to changing conditions, such as fewer funds than expected, changing political climate, or change in leadership.	1	2	3	4	5
	23. This group has the ability to survive even if it had to make major changes in its plans or add some new members in order to reach its goals.	1	2	3	4	5
Appropriate pace of development	24. This collaborative group has tried to take on the right amount of work at the right pace.	1	2	3	4	5
	25. We are currently able to keep up with the work necessary to coordinate all the people, organizations, and activities related to this collaborative project.	1	2	3	4	5

Factor	Statement	Strongly Disagree	Disagree	Neutral, No Opinion	Agree	Strongly Agree
Open and frequent communication	26. People in this collaboration communicate openly with one another.	1	2	3	4	5
	27. I am informed as often as I should be about what goes on in the collaboration.	1	2	3	4	5
	28. The people who lead this collaborative group communicate well with the members.	1	2	3	4	5
Established informal relationships and communication links	29. Communication among the people in this collaborative group happens both at formal meetings and in informal ways.	1	2	3	4	5
	30. I personally have informal conversations about the project with others who are involved in this collaborative group.	1	2	3	4	5
Concrete, attainable goals and objectives	31. I have a clear understanding of what our collaboration is trying to accomplish.	1	2	3	4	5
	32. People in our collaborative group know and understand our goals.	1	2	3	4	5
	33. People in our collaborative group have established reasonable goals.	1	2	3	4	5
Shared vision	34. The people in this collaborative group are dedicated to the idea that we can make this project work.	1	2	3	4	5
	35. My ideas about what we want to accomplish with this collaboration seem to be the same as the ideas of others.	1	2	3	4	5
Unique purpose	36. What we are trying to accomplish with our collaborative project would be difficult for any single organization to accomplish by itself.	1	2	3	4	5
	37. No other organization in the community is trying to do exactly what we are trying to do.	1	2	3	4	5
Sufficient funds, staff, materials, and time	38. Our collaborative group has adequate funds to do what it wants to accomplish.	1	2	3	4	5
	39. Our collaborative group has adequate "people power" to do what it wants to accomplish.	1	2	3	4	5
Skilled leadership	40. The people in leadership positions for this collaboration have good skills for working with other people and organizations.	1	2	3	4	5

Factors Score Sheet

Note: This score sheet allows for up to six different organizations to be involved. If the collaboration involves more organizations, copy the sheet and renumber the groups. Write the group's name at the top of each column. Enter the number of people from each organization who took the inventory where it says "n =". To get the "factor average" for that factor, first add the totals for all the statements about a particular factor and divide by "n". Then divide that number by the number of questions related to the factor. (If you are not keeping organization scores separately, use only the column marked "Whole Group.")

Here's an example:

Three raters complete The Wilder Collaboration Factors Inventory and want to know where their group stands in terms of "Flexibility." They consult the questionnaire and see that items eighteen and nineteen relate to this factor. Their individual ratings for these items are as follows:

	Item 18	Item 19
Rater 1	4	2
Rater 2	5	2
Rater 3	3	3

The raters follow steps (1) and (2) to yield an average score of 3.2 for "flexibility."

(1) $4 + 5 + 3 + 2 + 2 + 3 = 19$

(2) $19/6 = 3.2$

Note that all factors do not have the same number of questions. For example, "Ability to compromise" has only one question, while "Members share a stake in both process and outcome" has three questions. You will need to change the divisor in step (2) above to match the number of ratings for each factor.

To calculate scores on collaboration success factors as rated by the representatives of a specific organization within a collaborative group, simply follow steps (1) and (2) using only the ratings of individuals from the organization of interest. That is, add together all of the ratings by individuals from that organization and divide by the total number of ratings added.

Automatic scoring online

If you have access to the Internet, you can score this inventory online. Log on to the following URL and follow the instructions there: www.wilder.org/pubs/inventory/collaboration.html. If you have any trouble using this URL, please call the publisher at 1-800-274-6024.

Factor	State-ment	Whole Group n = ___	Group 1 n = ___	Group 2 n = ___	Group 3 n = ___	Group 4 n = ___	Group 5 n = ___	Group 6 n = ___
History of collaboration or cooperation in the community	1.							
	2.							
Factor average:								
Collaborative group seen as a legitimate leader in the community	3.							
	4.							
Factor average:								
Favorable political and social climate	5.							
	6.							
Factor average:								
Mutual respect, understanding, and trust	7.							
	8.							
Factor average:								
Appropriate cross section of members	9.							
	10.							
Factor average:								
Members see collaboration as in their self-interest	11.							
Factor average:								
Ability to compromise	12.							
Factor average:								
Members share a stake in both process and outcomes	13.							
	14.							
	15.							
Factor average:								
Multiple layers of decision-making	16.							
	17.							
Factor average:								
Flexibility	18.							
	19.							
Factor average:								
Development of clear roles and policy guidelines	20.							
	21.							
Factor average:								

Factor	State-ment	Whole Group n = ___	Group 1 n = ___	Group 2 n = ___	Group 3 n = ___	Group 4 n = ___	Group 5 n = ___	Group 6 n = ___
Adaptability	22.							
	23.							
Factor average:								
Appropriate pace of development	24.							
	25.							
Factor average:								
Open and frequent communication	26.							
	27.							
	28.							
Factor average:								
Established informal relationships and communications links	29.							
	30.							
Factor average:								
Concrete, attainable goals and objectives	31.							
	32.							
	33.							
Factor average:								
Shared vision	34.							
	35.							
Factor average:								
Unique purpose	36.							
	37.							
Factor average:								
Sufficient funds, staff, materials, and time	38.							
	39.							
Factor average:								
Skilled leadership	40.							
Factor average:								

Interpreting Your Scores

The Wilder Collaboration Factors Inventory does not have normative standards that would enable you to construct definitive interpretations of numerical scores for the factors. Instead, your scores on the inventory can be used as a basis for constructive discussion and planning for your collaborative initiative.

As a general rule, we would say:

- Scores of *4.0 or higher* show a strength and probably don't need special attention.
- Scores from *3.0 to 3.9* are borderline and should be discussed by the group to see if they deserve attention.
- Scores of *2.9 or lower* reveal a concern and should be addressed.

Here are some other things to consider when reviewing your results:

1) **What are the strengths and weaknesses of the collaborative group with respect to the factors that influence collaborative success?**

   While your scores on The Wilder Collaboration Factors Inventory do not describe your standing on the factors in absolute terms, they can serve as a relative indicator of your readiness to collaborate. Consider the three or four highest-rated factors for your organization, and for the group as a whole; these high-rated factors may represent strengths that your group can draw on to sustain collaboration, even in the face of major challenges. Similarly, the three or four lowest-rated factors may represent problem areas that your organization and collaborative group should take steps to address.

2) **Do representatives from all organizations in the collaborative group tend to rate the factors the same way? If not, what are the implications?**

   If you can, you should look not just at the scores on the factors as rated by the total group, but also at the scores as rated by each organization. If you see variances, the group should ask why these variances exist.

   Sometimes, an organization that sees things differently can provide valuable insight to the rest of the group. The representatives from that organization can lead the group to a very helpful new understanding of its strengths and weaknesses. For example, an organization that gives ratings much higher or lower than other organizations on "Skilled leadership" may have an important perspective on the group's leader (e.g., her ability to manage projects, her fairness or honesty, her experience in similar situations) that other organizations ought to understand.

   Other times, an organization that sees the factors very differently from its partners may be having trouble participating or may be "out of the loop" for important communications and does not understand what is going on. If this is the case, the group might use this discovery as an opportunity to take corrective action before serious problems develop.

3) For low-rated factors, are there particular items that are especially problematic?

It may be helpful to examine responses for individual items related to your group's lowest-rated factors. For instance, your group may have received a low-average score for "Sufficient funds, staff, materials, and time" because the group does not appear to have adequate funds (very low score for item thirty-eight), in spite of the fact that they have enough personnel (good score for item thirty-nine). When individual items are problematic, it is more efficient and effective to remedy the specific deficiencies than to attempt to improve your standing on the general factor.

4) How strong are your scores overall?

Your scores on The Wilder Collaboration Factors Inventory are *not* an absolute reflection of your group's ability to collaborate effectively. We cannot tell you how high your scores must be on each factor to ensure success, nor can we tell you that scores below a certain level will inevitably lead to failure. However, your scores can be used as a basis for commonsense judgments about how to proceed with your collaboration.

As suggested earlier, scores of 4.0 or higher probably indicate strength on a factor; scores 2.9 or lower probably should raise concern in your group. Scores from 3.0 to 3.9 ought to prompt some discussion on your part, to determine if you need to devote attention to them.

Here is some general advice to cover some situations in which you might find yourself:

- If any score falls below 3.0, you should have the group discuss this as soon as possible. You should develop a plan to remedy whatever problem(s) exist if you wish to proceed with the collaboration.

- If most of your group's scores fall in the middle of the rating scale (3.0 to 3.9), you may need to take steps to improve your standing on several factors before proceeding.

- If most scores fall at 4.0 or above, and just a few fall between 3.0 and 3.9, you can probably be confident that your group has no major shortcomings.

No matter what, however, do not be lulled into complacency by good scores. The factors require ongoing maintenance. For example, just because communication is good at the outset of an initiative does not mean that it will continue to be so, unless the collaborating partners make an effort to keep up such communication.

Understanding Collaboration

The term collaboration is used in many ways and has a variety of meanings to different people. Here's our working definition:

> **Collaboration** *is a mutually beneficial and well-defined relationship entered into by two or more organizations to achieve common goals.*
>
> *The relationship includes a commitment to mutual relationships and goals; a jointly developed structure and shared responsibility; mutual authority and accountability for success; and sharing of resources and rewards.*

In daily use, "collaboration" is often interchanged with "cooperation" and "coordination." We distinguish among the terms cooperation, coordination, and collaboration.

Cooperation is characterized by informal relationships that exist without any commonly defined mission, structure, or planning effort. **Coordination** is characterized by more formal relationships and understanding of compatible missions. **Collaboration** connotes a more durable and pervasive relationship. Collaborations bring previously separated organizations into a new structure with full commitment to a common mission. Such relationships require comprehensive planning and well-defined communication channels operating on many levels. Authority is determined by the collaborative structure. Risk is much greater because each member of the collaboration contributes its own resources and reputation. Resources are pooled or jointly secured, and the products are shared.

The Twenty Success Factors

Twenty factors influence the success of collaborations formed by nonprofit organizations, government agencies, and other organizations. The factors are grouped into six categories as follows:

Environment
   A. History of collaboration or cooperation in the community
   B. Collaborative group seen as a legitimate leader in the community
   C. Favorable political and social climate

Membership Characteristics
   A. Mutual respect, understanding, and trust
   B. Appropriate cross section of members
   C. Members see collaboration as in their self-interest
   D. Ability to compromise

Process and Structure
   A. Members share a stake in both process and outcome
   B. Multiple layers of participation
   C. Flexibility
   D. Development of clear roles and policy guidelines
   E. Adaptability
   F. Appropriate pace of development

Communication
   A. Open and frequent communication
   B. Established informal relationships and communication links

Purpose
   A. Concrete, attainable goals and objectives
   B. Shared vision
   C. Unique purpose

Resources
   A. Sufficient funds, staff, materials, and time
   B. Skilled leadership

1. Factors Related to the ENVIRONMENT

A. History of collaboration or cooperation in the community

A history of collaboration or cooperation exists in the community and offers the potential collaborative partners an understanding of the roles and expectations required in collaboration and enables them to trust the process.

B. Collaborative group seen as a legitimate leader in the community

The collaborative group (and, by implication, the agencies in the group) is perceived within the community as reliable and competent—at least related to the goals and activities it intends to accomplish.

C. Favorable political and social climate

Political leaders, opinion-makers, persons who control resources, and the general public support (or at least do not oppose) the mission of the collaborative group.

2. Factors Related to MEMBERSHIP CHARACTERISTICS

A. Mutual respect, understanding, and trust

Members of the collaborative group share an understanding and respect for each other and their respective organizations: how they operate, their cultural norms and values, their limitations, and their expectations.

B. Appropriate cross section of members

To the extent that they are needed, the collaborative group includes representatives from each segment of the community who will be affected by its activities.

C. Members see collaboration as in their self-interest

Collaborating partners believe that they will benefit from their involvement in the collaboration and that the advantages of membership will offset costs such as loss of autonomy and turf.

D. Ability to compromise

Collaborating partners are able to compromise, since the many decisions within a collaborative effort cannot possibly fit the preferences of every member perfectly.

3. Factors Related to PROCESS AND STRUCTURE

A. Members share a stake in both process and outcome

Members of a collaborative group feel "ownership" of both the way the group works and the results or products of its work.

B. Multiple layers of participation

Every level (upper management, middle management, operations) within each partner organization has at least some representation and ongoing involvement in the collaborative initiative.

C. Flexibility

The collaborative group remains open to varied ways of organizing itself and accomplishing its work.

D. Development of clear roles and policy guidelines

The collaborating partners clearly understand their roles, rights, and responsibilities, and they understand how to carry out those responsibilities.

E. Adaptability

The collaborative group has the ability to sustain itself in the midst of major changes, even if it needs to change some major goals, members, etc., in order to deal with changing conditions.

F. Appropriate pace of development

The structure, resources, and activities of the collaborative group change over time to meet the needs of the group without overwhelming its capacity, at each point throughout the initiative.

4. Factors Related to COMMUNICATION

A. Open and frequent communication

Collaborative group members interact often, update one another, discuss issues openly, and convey all necessary information to one another and to people outside the group.

B. Established informal relationships and communication links

In addition to formal channels of communication, members establish personal connections—producing a better, more informed, and cohesive group working on a common project.

5. Factors Related to PURPOSE

A. Concrete, attainable goals and objectives

Goals and objectives of the collaborative group are clear to all partners, and can realistically be attained.

B. Shared vision

Collaborating partners have the same vision, with clearly agreed-upon mission, objectives, and strategy. The shared vision may exist at the outset of collaboration, or the partners may develop a vision as they work together.

C. Unique purpose

The mission and goals, or approach, of the collaborative group differ, at least in part, from the mission and goals, or approach, of the member organizations.

6. Factors Related to RESOURCES

A. Sufficient funds, staff, materials, and time

The collaborative group has an adequate, consistent financial base, along with the staff and materials needed to support its operations. It allows sufficient time to achieve its goals and includes time to nurture the collaboration.

B. Skilled leadership

The individual who provides leadership for the collaborative group has organizing and interpersonal skills, and carries out the role with fairness. Because of these characteristics (and others), the leader is granted respect or "legitimacy" by the collaborative partners.

More results-oriented books available from Fieldstone Alliance

Collaboration Handbook
Creating, Sustaining, and Enjoying the Journey
by Michael Winer and Karen Ray

Shows you how to get a collaboration going, set goals, determine everyone's roles, create an action plan, and evaluate the results. Includes a case study of one collaboration from start to finish, helpful tips on how to avoid pitfalls, and worksheets to keep everyone on track.

192 pages, softcover   Item # 069032

Collaboration: What Makes It Work, 2nd Ed.
by Paul Mattessich, PhD, Marta Murray-Close, BA, and Barbara Monsey, MPH

An in-depth review of current collaboration research. Major findings are summarized, critical conclusions are drawn, and twenty key factors influencing successful collaborations are identified. Includes The Wilder Collaboration Factors Inventory, which groups can use to assess their collaboration.

104 pages, softcover   Item # 069326

Community Building: What Makes It Work
by Wilder Research Center

Reveals twenty-eight keys to help you build community more effectively. Includes detailed descriptions of each factor, case examples of how they play out, and practical questions to assess your work.

112 pages, softcover   Item # 069121

The Fieldstone Nonprofit Guide to
Conducting Community Forums
by Carol Lukas and Linda Hoskins

Provides step-by-step instruction to plan and carry out exciting, successful community forums that will educate the public, build consensus, focus action, or influence policy.

128 pages, softcover   Item # 069318

The Fieldstone Nonprofit Guide to
Developing Effective Teams
by Beth Gilbertsen and Vijit Ramchandani

Helps you understand, start, and maintain a team. Provides tools and techniques for writing a mission statement, setting goals, conducting effective meetings, creating ground rules to manage team dynamics, making decisions in teams, creating project plans, and developing team spirit.

80 pages, softcover   Item # 069202

The Fieldstone Nonprofit Guide to
Forming Alliances
by Linda Hoskins and Emil Angelica

Alliances don't have to be complex. This practical book helps you make the most of your resources by working with others.

112 pages, softcover   Item # 069466

The Nimble Collaboration
Fine-Tuning Your Collaboration for Lasting Success
by Karen Ray

Shows you ways to make your existing collaboration more responsive, flexible, and productive. Provides three key strategies to help your collaboration respond quickly to changing environments and participants.

136 pages, softcover   Item # 069288

The Nonprofit Mergers Workbook
The Leader's Guide to Considering, Negotiating, and Executing a Merger
by David La Piana

A merger can be a daunting and complex process. Save time, money, and untold frustration with this highly practical guide that makes the process manageable and controllable. Includes case studies, decision trees, twenty-two worksheets, checklists, tips, and complete step-by-step guidance from seeking partners to writing the merger agreement, and more.

240 pages, softcover   Item # 069210

View our entire catalog with pricing information or place an order at
www.FieldstoneAlliance.org

Fieldstone Alliance
60 Plato Boulevard East
Suite 150
Saint Paul, MN 55107

1-800-274-6024
www.FieldstoneAlliance.org

Printed in the USA
CPSIA information can be obtained
at www.ICGtesting.com
JSHW060050150824
68134JS00031B/2705